English as a Second Language

Graded Reader (Level 1)

Short Stories for Beginners

John Thompson

The Class Clown

Byeong what is standing up on one of the tables in the English lab at his middle school in his villiage in South Korea. He was known to his eighth grade class as a class clown.

A class clown likes to cut up or try to get other students to laugh by playing jokes, or miss behaving His teacher Mr. Thomas told him to sit down.

"Sit down!" Mr. Thomas yelled.

He was startled. He turned to jump down, but fell to the floor. The last thing he heard was a snap on his right leg.

The boy started to cry. He felt pain all through his body. The last thing he heard before painting was "help is on the way."

He woke up in the hospital. His mother was sitting on a chair beside his bed.

Byeong I asked his mother "what happened?"

"You're awake. So, how do you feel?"

"I feel terrible Mom. Does dad know?"

"Yes. I had to stop him from laughing when I told him. You know that at his work they don't like laughter."

"Why was he laughing?"

"Because he told you just last night that if you didn't stop clowning around at school, you would get hurt."

He started to cry. "I know that now, Mom. I just wish that I would've learned that before I got hurt."

The boy learned a valuable lesson after getting hurt there are rules at school for a reason. Teachers are not trying to make you have a tough time at school. They are trying to protect you.

Next time you think about breaking the rules, remember that rules are there to protect you.

After the accident, he still told jokes to friends in class, but he never again still on tables at school or did anything that could hurt him or others.

1. Who is Byeong and what was he doing in the English lab?

- Byeong is a middle school student in Byron South Korea. He was standing on one of the tables in the English lab.

2. How was Byeong known to his class?

- Byeong was known as a class clown who liked to cut up and make other students laugh by playing jokes or misbehaving.

3. What did Mr. Thomas tell Byeong to do?

- Mr. Thomas told Byeong to sit down.

4. What happened when Byeong tried to sit down?

- Byeong was startled and fell to the floor. He heard a snap on his right leg.

5. Where did Byeong wake up after the accident?

- Byeong woke up in the hospital.

6. Who was sitting beside Byeong's bed when he woke up?

- Byeong's mother was sitting beside his bed.

7. Why did Byeong's father laugh when he heard about the accident?

- Byeong's father laughed when he heard about the accident because he had warned Byeong the previous night that if he continued to clown around at school, he would get hurt.

-

8. What lesson did Byeong learn after getting hurt?

- Byeong learned that there are rules at school for a reason and that teachers are trying to protect students. He realized that he should follow the rules to avoid getting hurt or hurting others.

9. Did Byeong continue to tell jokes after the accident? What did he change?

- Yes, Byeong continued to tell jokes to his friends in class, but he never again stood on tables at school or did anything that could hurt him or others. He learned to follow the rules and behave appropriately in school.

The Bully

Jason Bromley was known at his middle school as a bully. He was only in the seventh grade. At 13 years old, he was in trouble at least once a week.

Today he was standing behind the school, trying to hurt a girl named Min-su.

"You need to go back to where you came from!" he shouted at her.

"I come from the USA."

"You don't look American."

"There isn't just one look in America. America is made up of many types of people."

She is right. In the USA there is not just one type of people. You can find Caucasian or white skin, or African Americans, Asian Americans, Arab Americans, and many others. The one thing that unites all people in the USA is that they are all Americans.

Most Americans were born in the USA, but son became an American during their lifetime.

"Well people like you should go to another country where they look like you," Jason said.

Jason pushed her down. Min-su started crying. When he saw her crying, he raised his fist to hit her.

That was when a boy in the eighth grade ran up and grabbed Jason space. He squeezed the arm of the bully, and then picked them up.

Kevin Wong was originally from China. His family became citizens of the USA when he was only five years old

From the time he was only seven, Kevin took a version of martial arts, called taekwondo. He had never used it at school before because it was only for defending himself.

Kevin put the bully down, hard enough, that the other boy was stunned, but not hurt.

"if you bully one more person, I will not be as gentle next time," he told him.

The bully ran to the front of the school. He knew that Kevin could've hurt him if he had wanted to.

"How can I thank you?", Min-su asked him.

"you don't have to thank me. I am glad you are safe."

If you ever have someone at school, they tried to bully you, tell your teachers. Tell your parents. If he or she keeps trying to hurt you, stand up in class, and shout it out. "stop it!"

A bully can only keep it up if no one stands up to them.

1. Who is Jason Bromley?
- Jason Bromley is a bully at a middle school.
2. How old is Jason Bromley?
- Jason Bromley is 13 years old.
3. Who was Jason trying to hurt behind the school?
- Jason was trying to hurt a girl named Min-su.
4. Where does Min-su come from?
- Min-su comes from the USA.
5. What did Jason say to Min-su?
- Jason told Min-su to go back to where she came from.
6. What did Kevin Wong do when he saw Jason raising his fist to hit Min-su?
- Kevin Wong ran up and grabbed Jason's arm to stop him.
7. What martial art did Kevin take from the age of seven?
- Kevin took taekwondo from the age of seven.

8. What did Kevin tell Jason after putting him down?
- Kevin told Jason that he wouldn't be as gentle next time if he bullied someone again.
9. What should you do if someone tries to bully you at school?
- You should tell your teachers and parents, and if the bullying continues, stand up in class and shout "stop it!"

The New Kid

Liam was excited to start at his new school. His family had moved across the country, and he was nervous about fitting in. But on his first day, he made friends quickly. Everyone was nice to him, except for one boy named Tyler.

Tyler was a big kid with a mean streak. He liked to make fun of other kids and push them around. Liam tried to ignore him, but Tyler kept singling him out.

One day, during recess, Tyler and his friends came up to Liam and started teasing him. They made fun of his clothes, his accent, and even his lunch. Liam didn't know what to do. He had never been bullied before.

But then, he remembered the advice his dad had given him before he started school. "If someone is bothering you, speak up. Don't let them get away with it."

So, Liam took a deep breath and stood up to Tyler. "Stop it, Tyler. I don't like the way you're treating me. It's not fair."

At first, Tyler just laughed. But then, something changed. Maybe it was the look on Liam's face, or the fact that he didn't back down. Tyler's friends started to drift away, and Tyler himself looked uncertain.

After a moment of silence, Tyler muttered, "Whatever, man. I was just joking." And he walked away.

Liam felt a rush of relief and pride. He had stood up to a bully and come out on top. And more importantly, he had shown Tyler that he wasn't going to be a victim.

From that day on, Tyler still acted tough sometimes, but he never bothered Liam again. And Liam felt more confident and secure in his new school.

The moral of the story is that standing up to bullies is important. It's not easy, but it's worth it. If you let bullies get away with their behavior, it will only get worse. But if you stand up to them, you can make a difference and show them that their behavior is not acceptable.

1. Who was Liam, and why was he nervous about his first day at school?

- Liam was a new student at a school he just moved to, and he was nervous about fitting in.

2. Who was the mean kid who kept singling Liam out at school?

- The mean kid was Tyler.

3. How did Tyler treat Liam?

- Tyler made fun of Liam's clothes, accent, and lunch.

4. What advice did Liam's dad give him before starting school?

- Liam's dad advised him to speak up if someone was bothering him and not to let them get away with it.

5. What did Liam do when Tyler and his friends were teasing him during recess?

- Liam stood up to Tyler and told him to stop.

6. How did Tyler react when Liam stood up to him?

- Tyler initially laughed, but then he and his friends drifted away, and Tyler looked uncertain.

7. What did Liam feel after standing up to Tyler?

- Liam felt a rush of relief and pride.

8. Did Tyler continue to bully Liam after Liam stood up to him?

- No, Tyler never bothered Liam again after Liam stood up to him.

9. What is the moral of the story?

- The moral of the story is that standing up to bullies is important, and it can make a difference.

Studying is Important

Yuri and Kang were both in the seventh grade at their middle school. They were good friends, but they were very different when it came to their approach to school.

Yuri loved to study. She spent hours each night reading her textbooks and doing her homework. She was always eager to learn new things and challenge herself. On the other hand, Kang didn't really care about school. He would often forget to do his homework and he rarely paid attention in class.

Despite their differences, Yuri and Kang remained good friends. But as the school year went on, Yuri started to pull ahead. She was getting all A's in her classes and was even recommended for an exclusive high school for gifted students.

Kang, on the other hand, was struggling. He was barely passing his classes and his teachers were starting to worry about him. Yuri tried to help him, but Kang just didn't seem interested.

One day, Yuri was studying at home when she got a text from Kang. "Hey, can you help me study for our math test tomorrow?"

Yuri was surprised but happy to help. They spent the next few hours going over the material together, and Kang seemed to be really engaged. He was asking questions and even coming up with his own strategies for remembering the formulas.

The next day, they both took the math test. Yuri knew she had done well, but she wasn't sure about Kang. After the test, they compared answers and Yuri was impressed. Kang had gotten almost everything right.

"I'm really proud of you, Kang," she said. "You did a great job."

Kang grinned. "Thanks, Yuri. I guess studying can actually be pretty helpful."

Over the next few weeks, Kang started to take school more seriously. He began doing his homework and paying attention in class. He even started to enjoy learning new things.

At the end of the school year, Yuri was accepted into the exclusive high school. She was thrilled, but she was also sad to leave Kang behind. However, Kang surprised her with a parting gift - a book on advanced calculus.

"I want to keep studying too," he said with a smile.

Yuri hugged him. "I'm proud of you, Kang. Keep it up."

The moral of the story is that studying is important. It may not always be fun or easy, but it can lead to great opportunities and personal growth. And with a little help and encouragement from friends, even those who don't like to study can learn to love it.

1. Who are the main characters in the story?
- The main characters in the story are Yuri and Kang.
2. What are their personalities like?
- Yuri likes to study and works hard to get good grades, while Kang doesn't enjoy studying and does not prioritize academics.
3. How does Yuri perform in school?
- Yuri gets all A's in school and is an excellent student.
4. What happened to Yuri after middle school?
- Yuri gets accepted into a special and exclusive high school.
5. Does Kang support Yuri's academic efforts?
- No, Kang does not support Yuri's academic efforts and often makes fun of her for being a "nerd".

6. What is the moral of the story?
- The moral of the story is that studying is important.
7. How does Yuri's hard work pay off in the end?
- Yuri's hard work pays off when she gets accepted into a special and exclusive high school.
8. What does Kang do when Yuri gets accepted into the special high school?
- Kang is surprised and somewhat envious of Yuri's achievement.
9. How does Yuri feel about her academic success?
- Yuri is proud of her hard work and academic success, but also feels sad that her friendship with Kang has suffered due to their different priorities.

Sportsmanship

Irving and Nelson were two seventh-grade boys who were always competitive with each other, especially when it came to sports. They were both on the school's soccer team, and they both wanted to be the best player.

During one game, Irving scored the winning goal, and he was thrilled. But as he celebrated, he noticed that Nelson looked upset. In fact, Nelson didn't even congratulate him on the win.

After the game, Irving went up to Nelson and asked him what was wrong. Nelson told him that he was disappointed that he didn't score the winning goal, and he felt like he had let the team down.

Irving realized that he had been so focused on winning that he hadn't even considered how Nelson might be feeling. He also realized that he didn't want to be the kind of person who only cared about winning and didn't care about his teammates' feelings.

So, Irving apologized to Nelson and told him that he was a great player and an important part of the team. He also told him that winning wasn't everything and that it was okay to not always come out on top if it meant turning into a rude person.

Nelson appreciated Irving's words, and from then on, they started to work together as a team instead of competing against each other. They both improved as players, and their team started to win more games.

The moral of the story is that competition in sports can sometimes bring out the worst in people, but it's important to remember that winning isn't everything. Being a good teammate and caring about others is more important than any trophy or medal.

1. Who are the main characters in the story?
- The main characters in the story are Irving and Nelson.
2. What grade are Irving and Nelson in?
- They are in 7th grade.
3. What lesson did Irving and Nelson learn about competition in sports?
- They learned that sometimes competition in sports brings out the worst in people.
4. What did winning mean to Irving and Nelson?
- Winning meant everything to Irving and Nelson. They were both very competitive and wanted to win at all costs.

5. How did Irving and Nelson's behavior change during the game?

- During the game, Irving and Nelson became very competitive and aggressive. They started to play dirty and were no longer playing for fun.

6. What did the coach say to Irving and Nelson after the game?

- The coach talked to Irving and Nelson after the game and told them that their behavior was unacceptable.

7. Did Irving and Nelson win the game?

- Yes, they won the game but they did not feel good about it.

8. What did Irving and Nelson realize after the game?

- After the game, Irving and Nelson realized that winning was not everything. They did not want to win if it meant turning into rude people.

9. What is the moral of the story?

- The moral of the story is that sometimes it is okay to not win, if winning means you turn into a rude person. It's important to remember that sports are supposed to be played for fun and not just to win.

Don't judge a book....

Carlos had always been a quiet kid. He was never really one to stand out in the crowd, and most of his classmates didn't really pay much attention to him. To them, he was just another face in the sea of middle school students.

But one day, something happened that changed everything. Carlos decided to audition for the school talent show.

Most of his classmates were surprised to hear that Carlos was going to perform. They didn't really know much about him, and they assumed that he probably wasn't very good at anything. But when Carlos took the stage and began to sing, the whole room was stunned.

It turns out that Carlos had an incredible singing voice. His voice was so powerful and so soulful that it brought tears to some of the students' eyes.

As he sang, the other students in the room realized that they had been wrong about Carlos. They had judged him based on his quiet nature and his unassuming appearance, but they had never taken the time to get to know him or see what he was capable of.

By the end of his performance, Carlos had won over the entire school. Everyone was talking about how amazing his voice was, and how they had never realized how talented he was.

From that day on, Carlos was no longer just another face in the crowd. He had proven himself to be an incredibly talented singer, and people began to see him in a new light.

The moral of the story is that you should never judge a book by its cover. Just because someone seems quiet or unassuming doesn't mean that they don't have hidden talents or abilities. It's important to take the time to get to know people and see what they're capable of before making assumptions about them. You never know, you might be pleasantly surprised by what you find out.

1. Who is the main character in the story?
- The main character in the story is Carlos.
2. How is Carlos treated by his classmates?
- Carlos is thought of as not important by his classmates.
3. What event does Carlos enter?
- Carlos enters a talent show.
4. What talent does Carlos have?
- Carlos can sing like a superstar.
5. How do the other students react when they hear Carlos sing?
- The other students are surprised and impressed when they hear Carlos sing.
6. What is the moral of the story?
- The moral of the story is to never judge a book by its cover.

7. What lesson can be learned from Carlos' experience?

- The lesson that can be learned from Carlos' experience is that everyone has hidden talents and abilities that should not be underestimated.

8. How does Carlos feel after the talent show?

- Carlos feels more confident and appreciated after the talent show.

9. How do Carlos' classmates treat him after the talent show?

- Carlos' classmates start to treat him with more respect and admiration after they discover his talent.

The Power of Kindness

Aiden was an 8th grader who loved to make people laugh. He would always tell jokes and pull pranks on his friends. But there was something that bothered him deep down. He noticed that some of the students in his school would make fun of others for no reason.

One day, Aiden witnessed a new student being teased by a group of boys. They were making fun of his clothes and his accent. Aiden felt bad for the new student and decided to do something about it.

He walked over to the group and said, "Hey guys, why are you making fun of him? He's new here, he doesn't know anyone."

The boys looked at Aiden like he was crazy. But Aiden didn't back down. He walked over to the new student and introduced himself. They started talking, and Aiden found out that the new student loved soccer, just like him.

From that day on, Aiden and the new student became good friends. They would hang out at lunch and talk about their favorite soccer teams. Aiden noticed that the other students in his school started to treat the new student better too. They saw that Aiden was friends with him and they realized that he wasn't so different after all.

The moral of the story is that kindness is powerful. A small act of kindness can make a big difference in someone's life. Aiden learned that sometimes, all it takes is one person to stand up for what is right and make a change.

1. **What is the title of the story? The title of the story is The Power of Kindness.**
2. **Who is the main character in the story?**
- **The main character in the story is Aiden, an 8th grader.**
3. **What is the good moral of the story?**
- **The moral of the story is to always do the right thing, even if it's not the popular or easy thing to do.**
4. **What is the problem that Aiden faces in the story?**
- **Aiden is faced with a situation where he has to decide whether to cheat on a test or not.**
5. **What does Aiden do when he is faced with the problem?**
- **Aiden decides not to cheat and instead studies hard for the test.**

6. How do Aiden's classmates react to his decision?

- Aiden's classmates are surprised by his decision, but they respect him for doing the right thing.

7. Does Aiden pass the test?

- Yes, Aiden passed the test because he studied hard and did not cheat.

8. How does Aiden feel after the test?

- Aiden feels proud of himself for making the right decision and passing the test on his own merit.

9. How does the story end?

- The story ends with Aiden feeling good about his decision and realizing that doing the right thing is always the best choice, even if it's not the easiest.

Travis, the Encourager

Travis was a special needs student in Wanda's 8th-grade class. He was always smiling, friendly, and loved to help others. Wanda, on the other hand, was going through a tough time at home. Her parents were going through a divorce, and she was struggling to cope with it all. She was often quiet and withdrawn in class, not participating in group activities or discussions.

One day, Travis noticed that Wanda was looking sad, and he decided to do something about it. He went up to her and asked if she was okay. At first, Wanda was hesitant to open up to Travis, but something about his friendly smile and genuine concern made her feel comfortable.

Travis listened patiently as Wanda shared her struggles. He didn't offer any advice, but he simply encouraged her and reminded her that she was strong and capable of getting through this tough time. He even shared some of his own challenges and how he had overcome them with the help of his family and friends.

Over the next few weeks, Travis made an effort to include Wanda in group activities and projects. He would often check on her and offer words of encouragement when she was feeling down. Wanda slowly started to open up more in class and even began to smile and participate in class discussions.

Through Travis's kindness and encouragement, Wanda started to believe in herself again. She realized that she didn't have to go through her struggles alone and that there were people like Travis who cared and were willing to help.

Travis's act of kindness and encouragement not only helped Wanda but also inspired the other students in the class to be more compassionate and supportive towards each other.

Moral of the story: Small acts of kindness and encouragement can make a big difference in someone's life.

1. **Who is the main character in the story?**
- The main character in the story is Travis, a special needs student.
2. **What is Travis known for in the story?**
- Travis is known for his kind and encouraging nature.
3. **Who does Travis encounter in the story?**
- Travis encounters Wanda, an 8th grader who is having trouble at home with her parents.
4. **How does Travis help Wanda in the story?**
- Travis encourages Wanda and reminds her to stay positive despite her troubles at home.
5. **What does Travis say to Wanda to lift her spirits?**
- Travis tells Wanda that she is strong and capable, and that she should focus on the things that make her happy.

6. How does Wanda initially react to Travis' encouragement?
- At first, Wanda is skeptical and unsure about Travis' words of encouragement.
7. What does Wanda do after talking with Travis?
- After talking with Travis, Wanda begins to feel more positive and hopeful about her situation.
8. What is the moral of the story?
- The moral of the story is that even those who are seen as different or special needs can offer valuable support and encouragement to others.
9. What can we learn from Travis' character in the story?
- From Travis' character, we can learn the importance of being kind, empathetic, and supportive towards others, regardless of their background or circumstances.

Saving Ricky

Ricky was an eighth-grader at Lincoln Middle School. He had moved to the United States with his family from Mexico when he was five years old. He was a great student and had made friends with everyone at school. He was always ready to help others and had a contagious smile that could brighten up anyone's day.

One day, Ricky's world was turned upside down. His family received a notice that their visas had expired, and they were to be deported back to Mexico. Ricky was devastated. He had spent most of his life in the United States and had no memory of his life in Mexico.

When the news spread throughout the school, everyone was in shock. Ricky's friends, including his classmates, teachers, and the principal, knew they had to do something to help him. They came together and formed a plan.

The students started a petition and organized a peaceful protest outside the school. They contacted local politicians and community leaders to spread awareness about Ricky's situation. They even started a GoFundMe page to help raise money for Ricky's legal fees.

The community rallied behind Ricky, and the news of his deportation gained attention from local news outlets. With the community's support, the case gained national attention, and Ricky's story was shared all over social media.

The support and love from the community gave Ricky and his family hope. They were granted a hearing to appeal their deportation, and their case was approved. The family could stay in the United States, and Ricky could continue his studies at Lincoln Middle School.

The experience brought the students closer together, and they learned the importance of standing up for what is right and the power of unity. Ricky's friends and classmates were proud of what they had accomplished and happy that their friend could stay in the country he had called home for most of his life.

The moral of the story is that we should always stand up for what is right, and together we can achieve great things. The power of unity can move mountains, and even the smallest act of kindness can make a big difference in someone's life.

1. Who is the protagonist of the story?
- The protagonist of the story is Ricky, a student at a middle school.
2. What is the problem faced by Ricky in the story?
- Ricky is facing the possibility of being deported to Mexico.
3. Why is Ricky in danger of being deported?
- Ricky is in danger of being deported because he and his family are undocumented immigrants.
4. How do the other students at the middle school feel about Ricky?
- The other students at the middle school are friends with Ricky and view him as a good student who deserves good things in life.
-

5. What do the students do to help Ricky?

- The students band together to protect Ricky from being deported. They create a petition to keep him in the country and spread awareness about his situation.

6. Who is the main leader of the effort to help Ricky?

- The main leader of the effort to help Ricky is a student named Maya.

7. How do the teachers and administrators at the school respond to the situation?

- Some teachers and administrators are supportive of the students' efforts to help Ricky, while others are hesitant or unsupportive.

8. Does the effort to help Ricky ultimately succeed?

- Yes, the effort to help Ricky ultimately succeeds, and he is able to stay in the country with his family.

9. What is the moral of the story?
- The moral of the story is that people should stand up for what is right and help others in need, even if they are facing difficult circumstances or opposition.

Printed in Great Britain
by Amazon

37511997R00040